ISLE OF MAN STEAM RAILWAY

One of the two locomotives rostered for the day's work was 1885 built 0-6-0T locomotive CALEDONIA (MNR No.4), which was photographed in Douglas station with the 09.50 train to Port Erin on Thursday 12/9/2019.

The façade / main building of Douglas station which was built as part of a station upgrade between 1889 and 1891 is built in the Victorian Gothic style using Ruabon red bricks.

A profile view of CALEDONIA going on shed at Douglas for servicing prior to working the evening pie and mash train of Thursday 12/9/2019. The photo was taken from the signal box steps during an escorted visit.

CALEDONIA at Ballasalla station with the 09.50 Douglas to Port Erin service on Thursday 12/9/2019.

The other loco of the day was No.8 FENELLA (built by Beyer Peacock in 1894 as BP3610) which is viewed at Ballasalla with the 10.00 Port Erin to Douglas service on a damp 12/9/2019. This train crossed the CALEDONIA hauled 09.50 Douglas to Port Erin train at Castletown.

At Port Erin station which is the 'southerly' end of the Isle of Man Steam Railway route, the recently arrived MNR No.4 CALEDONIA is seen by the water crane having been serviced ready for its return journey to Douglas (the 16.00 from Port Erin) on 12/9/2019.

No.16 MANNIN of 1926 (BP6296) was photographed in the Museum at Port Erin in September 2019, the loco has since been removed from the museum in early 2020 with a view to returning it to steam again by 2023 for The Isle of Man Railway 150th. MANNIN was the largest and most powerful of the 2-4-0 tanks and was bought especially to work the heavily loaded holiday trains on the undulating Douglas to Port Erin route.

The wraps were lifted off of No.1 SUTHERLAND, which was undergoing cosmetic restoration at Douglas on 12/9/2019, prior to being moved to Port Erin museum to replace No.16.

During a guided tour around Douglas workshops at the end of the day, No. 12 HUTCHINSON (Beyer Peacock 5126 of 1908) was seen at the back of the running shed awaiting overhaul and was sharing space with some of the diesel fleet on 12/9/2019.

The chassis of the 1874 Beyer Peacock built No.4 LOCH (BP1416) undergoing overhaul in the machine shop area in Douglas workshops which themselves were built circa 1891.

'One' of the County Donegal Railcars, consisting of number 19's coach which is paired with number 20's cab is seen in the workshops at Douglas. The two railcar's Gardner 6LW engines were overhauled some years ago by Gardners and this cab body is clearly the subject of some remedial work involving new timber framing and re-skinning. Photo taken 12/9/2019.

Narrow Gauge Class 58 lookalike No.21 which was built by Motive Power and Equipment Solutions Inc of the USA in 2013 is seen in the company of an unidentified Wickham permanent way vehicle in the running shed at Douglas on 12/9/2019.

Hunslet Engine Company 4wDM (22021 of 1994) was once used on Jubilee Line tunnelling operations before coming to the Isle of Man to become their No.18, it is used for shunting duties at Douglas and is named AILSA.

Schottler 0-4-0DH loco 2175 of 1958 in the shed at Douglas and is now known as No.17 VIKING; this locomotive was purchased by the Isle of Man Railway in 1992 for use as:- a general shunter, permanent way train duties and to haul the occasional passenger train in times of emergency.

MANX ELECTRIC RAILWAY

Unvestibuled saloon No.1 of 1893 and 1895 built trailer No.59 (which were both built by Milnes) form a special Bluebell Railway charter service to Ramsey on Friday the 13/9/2019 and are seen during a photo stop at Laxey. Trailer No.59 is known as the Royal Saloon (due to conveying Edward the Seventh in 1902) and is painted in its original Douglas and Laxey Electric Tramway livery

Left: MER vestibuled saloon No.7 of 1894 at Derby Castle prior to working the 11.40 service to Ramsey on Wednesday 11/9/2019. Car No. 7 was used by the OHL department and the permanent-way department for a number of years and degenerated to a very poor condition. In 2007, this car was removed from 'duties' and extensively rebuilt and made its return in 2011. When it returned to traffic, it was in a deep blue, white and teak colour scheme, which was that of the Douglas & Laxey Electric Tramway when the tramway first opened.

Right: Winter saloon No.20 passing The Mines pub at Laxey in bright sunshine with the 11.40 Ramsey to Douglas on 14/9/2019.

Tram 5 + trailer cross the main road at Laxey near The Mines pub with the 10.10 Ramsey to Douglas service on Saturday 14/9/2019.

The permanent way train with Motor Rail Simplex 40S280 of 1966 at its head in the siding at Laxey. Photo taken 14/9/2019.

The Bluebell Railway's charter special which utilized tram No.1 and trailer No. 59 'on the blocks' at the new Ramsey terminus on 13/9/2019.

An unusual view of the former Ramsey tram terminus from the top of Leyland PD3a double decker bus No.67 which was chartered by our group to 'explore' the west side of the island. Photo taken 13/9/2019.

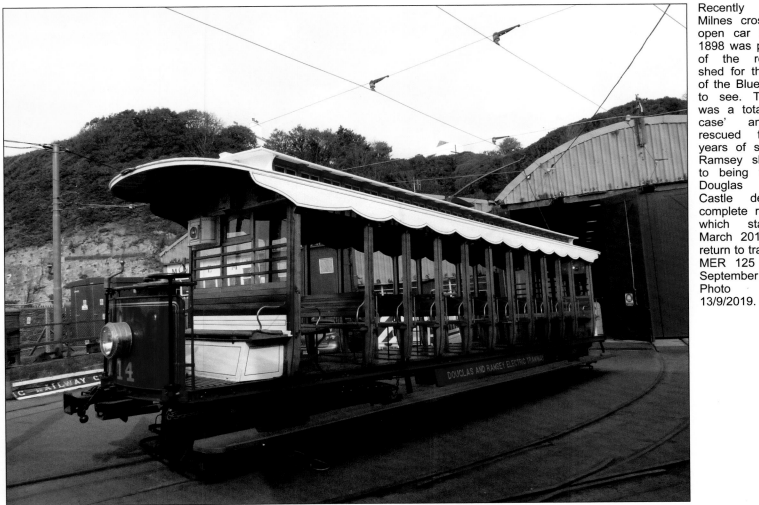

Recently restored Milnes cross bench open car No.14 of 1898 was pulled out of the restoration shed for the benefit of the Bluebell party to see. This tram was a total 'basket case' and was rescued from 20 years of storage in Ramsey shed prior to being towed to Douglas Derby Castle depot for complete restoration which started in March 2015 with a return to traffic at the MER 125 event of September 2018. Photo taken 13/9/2019.

3 car line-up in the tram storage/running shed at Derby Castle. From left to right:- numbers 6, 56 and 43, 9 was in the shed next door.

Machine tools and tool equipment in the main workshop at Derby Castle. Note the belt drives.

This yellow cabin is part of the motor test area and is fitted with a glass roof for observation of the resistor grids above it which are used for electrical loading when a motor is on test.

Winter saloon No.21 with its bogies off, over the pit in the workshop area at Derby Castle.

One of the original two Milnes cars (No. 2) of 1893 is seen in the workshop area at Derby Castle.

Philip (A Strawberry Roan Clydesdale) and tram car 45 photographed by another Philip at Derby Castle towards the end of the day on Saturday 14/9/2019.

DOUGLAS HORSE TRAMWAY

Douglas (A Bay Clydesdale) and tram car 45 plus driver outside the Best Western Hotel on the seafront at Douglas on 11/9/2019.

A view of Douglas seafront at 08.20 showing the new track alignment and ongoing tramway rebuild down the centre of the promenade road on Friday 13/9/2019; the temporary horse tramway terminus was right outside the Best Western Hotel.

Inside the horse stables during a visit in the afternoon of Monday 16/9/2019 with 'Trammers' Nelson (left) and William (right) posing for the camera! The stable complex dates from 1877 and is now a listed heritage building in its own right.

The 'new' replica horse tram car sheds under construction at Derby Castle on 16/9/2019.

The temporary horse tram car shed at Derby Castle on 16/9/2019 with tram 29 inside.

SNAEFELL MOUNTAIN RAILWAY

Left: Snaefell tram No.5 arrives at Laxey with the 11.10 service from the Summit on 13/9/2019.

Right: 3 tram line up at Laxey on Wednesday the 11/9/2019. From L to R:- No.5 in the current livery, No.1 in the original livery and tram 20 and trailer 41 on the 13.40 Douglas to Ramsey. By careful scrutiny, it may be just possible to detect the difference in the 2 track gauges present at Laxey. (ie 3'6" & 3')

Snaefell cars 1 and 5 at Laxey with No.5 looking fully loaded and ready to make its journey to the summit on 14/9/2019.

Snaefell tram number 1 in the original blue livery of 1895 at the Summit and ready to form the 13.40 service to Laxey on the 11/9/2019. It is often said that from the top of this 2036 feet high mountain, you can see 7 Kingdoms! (But I won't list them here)

Left: Tram No.5 departs the Summit with the 13.10 to Laxey on the 11/9/2019.

Right: Tram No.1 arriving at the Summit with the 13.15 from Laxey on 11/9/2019.

GROUDLE GLEN RAILWAY

Left: 1896 built Bagnall locomotive number 1484 SEA LION is seen running round its train at Sea Lion Rocks station at 11.35 am on Sunday the 15/9/2019.

Right: New build replica Bagnall SIPAT design 0-4-0ST OTTER of 2018 departing Lhen Coan station at 12.15 for Sea Lion Rocks station on the 15/9/2019. This locomotive was built by the North Bay Railway engineering works in Darlington. The Groudle Glen Railway, which re-opened in 1986 has always wanted 3 operational steam locomotives and this was certainly portrayed during the visit of the Bluebell party.

Left: New build Bagnall pattern loco BROWN BEAR which was built between 2013 and 2019 arrives with a train at Sea Lion Rocks station. This loco entered traffic on the G G R in July 2019 and is a pattern of the 1905 built loco Polar Bear which 'lives' at Amberley in Sussex.

Right: The driver of OTTER exchanges the token with the driver of SEA LION in the passing loop near Sea Lion Rocks station at around 13.35 on the 15/9/2019.

Left: Hudson-Hunslet locomotive DOLPHIN works number 4352 of 1952 in the workshop at Lhen Coan. DOLPHIN and WALRUS were built together by the Hunslet Engine Co on behalf of Robert Hudson Ltd and were originally supplied to the Tilbury Contracting and Dredging Co. Ltd. After several more owners, they were purchased by the GGR in 1983.

Right: Hudson-Hunslet locomotive WALRUS works number 4353 of 1952 in the workshop with a newly varnished carriage.

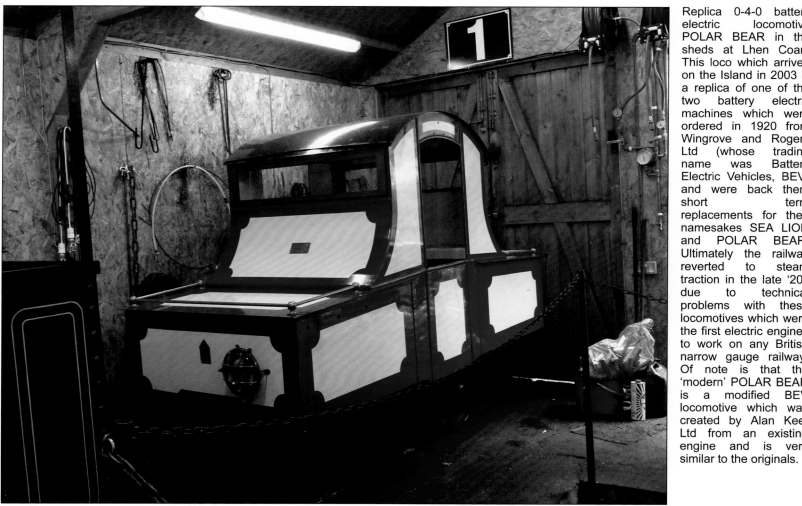

Replica 0-4-0 battery electric locomotive POLAR BEAR in the sheds at Lhen Coan. This loco which arrived on the Island in 2003 is a replica of one of the two battery electric machines which were ordered in 1920 from Wingrove and Rogers Ltd (whose trading name was Battery Electric Vehicles, BEV) and were back then, short term replacements for their namesakes SEA LION and POLAR BEAR. Ultimately the railway reverted to steam traction in the late '20s due to technical problems with these locomotives which were the first electric engines to work on any British narrow gauge railway. Of note is that the 'modern' POLAR BEAR is a modified BEV locomotive which was created by Alan Keef Ltd from an existing engine and is very similar to the originals.

GREAT LAXEY MINES RAILWAY

A 2 loco line up at the Laxey Gardens terminus of the G L M R on Saturday the 14/9/2019. On the left is BEE on the service train and on the right is WASP which wasn't in service on this day. The driver consults his watch just prior to the train's departure at 13.15.

Left: ANT undergoing maintenance outside the loco shed at Laxey Gardens depot on 14/9/2019. The old sheds were repaired for re-use when the railway was re-instated.

Right: BEE propels the man rider towards the tunnel mouth on its way to the Great Laxey Mine station at 13.16 on the 14/9/2019. This tunnel is the longest on the Isle of Man and runs under the Laxey to Ramsey road.

Left: A general view of Laxey Gardens station, taken from the road above on 14/9/2019. WASP, which is a 0-4-0 battery electric loco was built by Claytons in 1973 and is coupled to a man rider whilst being stored in the second platform because it was not in use on this day.

Right: The view of the depot area at Laxey Gardens depot showing the former ore washing and crushing area to the right; the photograph was taken from above the tunnel on 14/9/2019.

BEE and man rider depart the Great Laxey Mine station at 12.35 on 14/9/2019. This 19" gauge railway was reopened in September 2004 and is a reconstruction of the surface section (a quarter mile long) of the Great Laxey Mine tramway which ran from the mine adits and carried lead and zinc laden ore to the processing floors at Laxey. The original tracks above the ground, plus locomotives and stock were scrapped around the mid 1930s.

GREAT LAXEY MINE RAILWAY

A profile view of ANT outside the loco shed at Laxey Gardens depot on 14/9/2019. This locomotive and BEE are replicas of the original engines which were built by the Stephen Lewin Engineering Co. of Poole circa 1877. The new ANT and BEE were built by Great Northern Steam Ltd of Darlington during 2004.

THE ORCHID LINE

The Orchid Line at Curraghs Wildlife Park which is operated by the Manx Steam and Model Engineering Club opened their line especially for the Bluebell Railway party on 13/9/2019. 0-6-0T + tender ROBERT EDWARD is seen passing through the main station on a track inspection run.

A busy time on the Orchid Line, this required 2 trains in service to carry the volume of passengers. Framed between the water cranes are (left) 0-6-0T + tender ROBERT EDWARD and (right) Class 47 ODIN.

Left: Class 47 look-a-like ODIN passes through the main station with a light load on the Orchid Line on 13/9/2019. The loco was built by the club in 2012 and is both petrol electric and battery electric powered.

Right: 0-6-0T + tender ROBERT EDWARD passes under the footbridge near the meerkat colony during the afternoon of Friday 13/9/2019.

LNER 2-6-0T 1510 on an elevated work platform in the shed/depot at the Orchid Line on the 13/9/2019.

Schools Class loco 30940 with 0-6-0 diesel No.6 MAURICE behind, seen in the shed at the Orchid Line.

RAILWAY RELICS

At the entrance to Curraghs Wildlife Park is a small section of track still embedded in a level crossing which was once part of the Manx Northern Railway line to Ramsey; this route was closed in September 1968! However between 1965 and the closure date, there was a halt called Ballavolley where passengers could alight for the Wildlife Park. This view is looking towards St Johns which was the junction station for Peel.

Whilst not on the current operational railway, there is a very well laid out mini museum/display at what was the throat of Peel station (Mill Road) which is seen to full effect in sunshine on Tuesday 17/9/2019. The museum is known as the Manx Transportation Museum and 'contains' a signal which was re-located from Lezayre on the Manx Northern Line and the carriage body C1 that was built by the Metropolitan Railway Carriage and Wagon Company in 1873 and became part of bogie 3rd carriage No.64 in 1912. The water tower is original as is the former Brick Works office opposite which houses a varied display of items including a P50 bubble car which was built locally.

The Ramsey Pier train's baggage truck and carriage No.2028. The baggage truck is one of the originals and the carriage was purchased in 1937 along with the locomotive.

The Ramsey Pier Railway's 3' gauge Planet locomotive No. 2027 of 1937 and carriage 2028 on 17/9/2019. When delivered, this locomotive had an 8hp motor but was subsequently replaced by a much larger Ford V4 motor! Insets: Top, the original works plate. Bottom, the replacement motor.

The Upper Douglas Cable Tramway (which operated from 1896 to 1929) car seen here was rebuilt from parts of former trams 72 and 73 and carries a different number at each end to belie the fact! This vehicle is now located at the Jurby Transport Museum (which opened in 2010) but was once the core of a bungalow in Jurby village until 1976; the restored cable car was photographed during a visit to the museum on 17/9/2019. Inset Top, the controller which was added along with an electric motor underneath (not shown) to allow the tram to run off of batteries (when fitted).